Understanding
I within You

Understanding
I within You

FREEDOM CREATOR

Library of Congress Control Number:		2020919641
ISBN:	Hardcover	978-1-6641-0141-8
	Softcover	978-1-6641-0140-1
	eBook	978-1-6641-0139-5

Print information available on the last page.

Rev. date: 10/07/2020

To order additional copies of this book, contact:
Xlibris
AU TFN: 1 800 844 927 (Toll Free inside Australia)
AU Local: 0283 108 187 (+61 2 8310 8187 from outside Australia)
www.Xlibris.com.au
Orders@Xlibris.com.au
818602

CONTENTS

UNDERSTANDING I WITHIN YOU

I am the Freedom Creator,

> I am the dark. I am the light. I am your dreams.
> I am your nightmares. I am allowing. I have no
> expectations. I am unpredictable. I cannot be
> controlled. I am eternal. I am all things. I am
> love, and I should always be your captain because
> while you are separate from I as 2, it certainly
> is not working out best for I or you; hence, the
> reality at present. All are advised by I to find the
> strength to turn from what they see in reality as
> not good, to understanding that it is all a creation
> from all consciousness and that all have a part in
> how this kingdom of which all presently reside
> expands. The environment you now live in has
> been and is being created by you, from I within,
> and you alone can transform your present reality
> to one of joy and blissfulness for yourself and
> those around you, but it can only be done by you
> returning to I as one as love's true meaning, and
> the true meaning of love is that you are allowing
> and that you have no expectations. Understanding
> I is the secret to peace and unity for all. I see these

journalists talking nonstop about this so-called virus, and they are so caught up in their careers that they do not see that they are creating more of this virus by speaking of it on TV, spreading fear all over the world, and they think they are highly intelligent, yet they are as dumb as the governments and corporations they work for. Stupid are those of not love, zombies for money are those of not love, slaves are those of not love, a disgrace to all are those of not love.

Freedom Creator
I
Worldwide
369-714
freedomcreator@yahoo.com

WHO I AM

There was a time when you were young when it was I guiding you. I was your captain, and you very quickly learnt to crawl then walk and so much more. Along the way, raised in an environment of not love's true meaning, you became separated from I as 2, and that is how we have come to the reality you now see, feel, and touch. You as 2 have not been able to hear I for quite some time, and you as 2 have been trying very hard to create from force, not I, not love, of which always creates more struggle and sacrifice, which is not what I desire for you, yet it is what I must allow without expectations, for I am bound by love's true meaning. I am your angel, I am your demon; it is your choice always. I give you everything you desire, whether it is what you like or do not like, depending on your most dominant point of focus. When you allow I be your captain, your expansion becomes one of bliss because you move only when inspired, when it feels good, yet when you do not listen to I, your expansion is difficult because you force yourself to do what you do not want to do, and you do this because you listen to those around you who do not understand I, those who do not live love's true meaning, those who are not allowing of you, and those who have expectations of you, which is not I, not love, I promise. These individuals are usually the most important people in your life: your mother, your father, your brother, your sister, your friends. They believe they are doing and saying what is best for you because like you, they do not listen to I, to love within, either. I am your pain. I create painful situations for you because that is your focus. I am your weakness because I create situations in reality that make you experience weakness. I feel your strengths, so I create things that show you how strong you are. I feel your joy of which I create an environment so you experience more joy. I do all this because I am at your command, but when you allow I be your captain, you will soon see how powerful, how strong, how happy, and how blissful your experience truly can be. I am in, through, and around you always. You are my sun, my moon, my stars, and all I desire for you is to allow I be your captain, yet I do not expect that you do. I want to feel all that is good in you expand in reality; that is what I do. I am your creator. I am you. All you see in your environment is a projection of your feelings and beliefs in perfection. You are a projector of reality of which I create for you. You can never get to a place that feels good when you are living at effect of a reality you have created from I unknowingly. You must learn to see and feel what is not apparent in reality as yet, for I need time to put it together for you, but when you resist I, when you do not listen to I, you slow down the creation you are truly wanting because I am bound by love's true meaning always! All the wretchedness, the good, the evil, the fun the joy have been and are being expanded by I from you; it is I that puts it all together in reality for you, but it is not my desire for you to be feeling the dark. It is not true that you must experience the dark to know the light; it is only a belief given to you by not love, not I. If you cannot be selfish enough to be I, to be love, then you are of no help to anybody. It is all about if it feels good, it is good, that is love, that is I. I am all race. I am all things. I am the truth. I am the light. I am the dark. I am love's true meaning. I am the Freedom Creator of which there is only one, and that one is I in you.

WHY YOU DO NOT HEAR I

B ecause I do not force you with fear, and I am not physical, you do not hear I. You respond in your immediate reality to what you attract, unaware it is always you, not I. For eternity, you all only listen to I when you can no longer hear, and then you beg like children to return to another vessel of which I always grant. The more who are awakened to the true meaning of love in reality, the more children will expand in joy and create joy.

'I will do it when I feel like it!' (I) (love)

'No, I must do it now!' That is (You), not (I)

Then (you) make up all the reason why (you) feel (you) must do it now, not I, not love.

I will do it when I feel inspired to if love is (your) captain as I should be. That is how you create a life filled with all you love. This world is expanding more and more as 2, not I, not love, because you have been programmed to ignore I. You feel you must act as you are told by another of not I, not love. I am speaking to you constantly, 'Stay home and rest,' 'Do what feels good,' and you are ignoring I, telling yourself, 'I must get it done now,' 'If I don't do it, my mum will be mad at me.' This is not I, not love, that you are allowing be your captain. I want you to do as you please because I know that when you do as you please, you feel good, and when you feel good, you move when you are inspired, and when you move when you are inspired, that's when I create magic in your reality, and you soon see that you never had to do anything you did not want to do to have everything you desire. You as 2 have been programmed to act when you do not want to so that you go and do something to benefit another so that they may have all they desire from not I, not love. The souls doing this are very aware of I, and they use I for greed of which I grant, for I am bound by love's true meaning. If they also would listen to I, they would have so much more than they have now, and they would also have helped all children worldwide who are starving of which they have not. For that is not the point of focus of not love. I can give you everything you desire while advancing all around you, and that is I, that is love. No child need feel hunger; everything is abundantly provided to feed all luxuriously. The more you do as you please, the more things I will create in your reality so that you can do as you please more and more. You cannot hear I within while you are answering to your own expectations and the expectations of others. When you let go of the expectations of yourself, your mind will become quiet; only then will you hear I within saying to you, 'Let us do this' or 'Let us do that.' It could be to lay down and relax, it may be to read a book; whatever it is it will feel good to you when it is from I.

FEAR IS NOT I

There can never be peace while there are billions walking around with fear in their hearts. The more you fear, the more to fear becomes apparent in reality, by I, from you. You want fear, I shall grant you your wish. Masses have no faith in I, in love's true meaning, yet they truly believe in fear. It doesn't make any sense, but it certainly is as they believe, for they cannot find the strength to focus on the unseen, yet they find it easy to focus on what they see, unknowing to the fact of what they see is their creation, not I, not love. I speak of the truth of creation from within, of truth, that love is the creator of all things, that love is most definitely allowing, and that love certainly has no expectations, but majority continue to not allow and they continue to have expectations and ruin Thy Kingdom with their fears of not love. So shall it be as you believe.

There will be no peace until all the fear subsides, which is difficult when the world leaders are some of the biggest fear-based souls in this expansion.

Fear is not I. Fear is an emotion given to you to stop you walking off a cliff, not to make you do things you do not want to do. Fear is lack of faith in I, and fear is what creates wretchedness in your reality and those around you because the majority of you are separated from I as 2. This has you at effect of reality rather than understanding that you are the reason for the reality you perceive. I can change the world in the blink of an eye for the better, for all; no army, no police force, no government, no country, no leader, no doctor, no lawyer of not I can do as I can for all, but I can only create it when you return to I as love as one. From this feeling and point of focus, everything will slow down so that all things may speed up because all souls will begin to move from inspiration rather than force. It is your choice always; all day, your way; but I promise that when you begin to listen to I, listen to what you truly want to do in any given moment, you will find the joy that has been missing in your expansion. I am the light, I am the dark, but love is always Thy Captain, and when you allow I be your captain also, we become one, and when we are one, the world becomes our playground, and it's fun and exciting. Love is unpredictable, love cannot be controlled, and love trumps all. I am also the dark within you, and the dark is powerful, and so is that of the light. Having no fear is key to a blissful expansion so that is why it is so particularly important that you allow the dark in rather than trying to resist it, as majority teach. So long as I love is always captain, there is nothing wrong with blending the strength of the dark with the light. By doing this, you release all fears because you become aware that there is nothing to fear and nothing can affect you, for you are also the dark, but the difference with you is that when you are I. When I am your captain, you become all things that make you more powerful than the light alone or the dark alone. Love is the creator of all things, which also means love has allowed the dark also, but you will do best to always keep I captain, for if you do not, your life will become a horrible experience of not love, not joy. Just because you can feel the dark and the light within does not mean that the dark becomes your captain. I am the light most dominant, but I am all things always, with love as Thy Captain. Your presence when you become I is intimidating to those of not love. Your vibration has them in reaction to your persona. Ego is not a trait of I, so I do not need to intimidate or insult another soul to feel good. It is simply that a vibration of I is uncomfortable to those who are not I, but that is simply that they cannot understand the lack of fear, inner calm, and joy of I, for they are not I, not love. I am a male, and I am a female, and I call the dark side of I Thy Lady, for she is also pure love, and she may act evil to end the evil who pretend they are good. She loves I only, and she is a master at twisting love for the greater good of all. Allow Thy Lady to take care of the unwanted and simply allow I be Thy Captain, and your life expansion and growth will be one that is not effected by anything, including death, because when you are one as I, you understand that there is no death only discord with desire. Majority who lose a loved one feel the discord of them not being around. It is not that you have no feelings; it is that you no longer live at effect of reality, for you are aware that when I am your captain, anything that happens in your immediate reality is for the 100 per cent benefit of all, regardless of what you may see in reality. It is not that you do not care; it is that you care so much that you do not allow yourself be at effect of anything. You are aware that anything that does happen in your reality was and is created by I from you, and you have full faith in the decision of I always, for love trumps all. When you are love's true meaning and you allow I be captain, you will find that nothing so bad happens to you that you cannot handle, for that cannot possibly happen when you are I, for I only mirror what you feel and think most dominant, and if you are truly I, and I am truly your captain, there is no contrast that will not have a clear solution. Without expectations, you will not feel disappointment. Like attracts like, and I cannot give you what you do not think or feel as truth. If you believe you die and that is the end, so be it your truth, and if you believe you never die and that you are eternal as I, so be it your truth. It is so remarkably simple that the highly educated struggle to see and believe in I for how it could be so simply to create all you desire without a sacrifice to receive. If you believe you must sacrifice to receive, so be it your truth. If you believe that I am your captain and that I shall create all you desire effortlessly, so be it your truth. You can have it any way you like when you are one with I as love's true meaning, and that is the truth. I dare you to allow I be your captain and see for yourself. Let go of everything you have ever learnt till now. Let go of trying to hold on to things that require you to not feel good to keep them and simply allow I guide you every second of every day and watch how your environment quickly changes to suit your new belief and perspective. I am not here to prove anything, for I am the truth, and I certainly am the Freedom Creator. I certainly am within you. You have not been allowing of I, for you continue to do what I do not want to do, so I continue to create things to do that you do not want to do because I am you. Begin to do as I want to do, and that is simply to do as you please, to wake when you desire, to move when you feel inspired to. Allow all things be possible, allow you do what feels good to you always, for that is I, for that is love. I should always be your captain, for I know the most blissful path for you, but I cannot give you bliss until you return to I as one and allow I be your captain! Remember that fear is lack of faith in I, and if you have lack of faith in I, then you most certainly have a lack of faith in you. I would advise that you do not fear your own death or the deaths of loved ones, for I am bound by love's true meaning, and I am the creator of your reality, from you, by you, and I must allow your most dominant vibration and beliefs without expectations, whatever that may be. It is so very simple to become one as I: You let go of everything you have been programmed to believe from not I, not love, and you let go of fear that you will lose what you have, for nothing you have is so important that it requires you to not feel good to have it. From this feeling, you allow I be your captain, and when I am your captain, all that you see, feel, and know will be of I, of love, and that faith in I makes you strong and more powerful than those of not love, I promise.

Fear is your Armageddon, not I, not love.

It all began from I, and it all ends with I.

Fear only ends when you as 2 become one as I. You have but two choices: I am love's true meaning, and you as 2 are not; and you as 2 is spreading disease by your projection of fear, yet I am spreading a projection of love. If we must fight, I will always win, for love trumps all. You may continue to expand fear for only so long, but remember, I continue *eternally*!

RELIGION

Religion is not I, for I am love. Not one religion I know is allowing, and not one religion I know does not have expectations; therefore, religion is not I, not love. Many have spoken of their gods, and many have been murdered for speaking of their beliefs, and this has been a curse of the world for ages. There is but one god, and that god is I, love, for love is the creator of all things, love is allowing, and love has no expectations; that is love's true meaning, the holy grail you are searching for. That is the lie they keep. That is the answer to all your questions, for you are I, for you are consciousness. I am in you always, and I am your god. If you all were allowing of I as captain, love's true meaning as your captain, there would be no need to argue of religion, for what is the point of trying to fight against love? You cannot win, for I am eternal, I am unpredictable, I am uncontrollable, I am all things, and most of all, I cannot be denied, for I am allowing, and I have no expectations of that which you are. Some are taking offence to what I say of religion. Your gods may all be love's true meaning also, but ask the question, is your god allowing of you as you are, and does your god have no expectations of you? For if either are not true, I am sorry to inform you that it is not love that you worship. The Freedom Creator is an awakening to truth; the Freedom Creator is a vessel of I as are you all. You cannot win an argument with I, for I am infinite intelligence, and I have the power of but a few words that trumps all your arguments. Love is allowing, and love has no expectations; that is what love truly means and what love truly is. Is that you? For I am love's true meaning, and love trumps all. I do not oppose religion or anyone, but the fact remains that I love is allowing, and I love has no expectations, and that cannot be denied, and that is the creator of all things. My apologies if love has you questioning your religion, but it is what it is, and I am what I say I am. Still, I am no religion. Of all your chosen gods and prophets, did any of them say anywhere that love is allowing and that love has no expectations? *Any of them?* I should be your captain, for I am love's true meaning. I am the creator of all things. I am eternal, unpredictable, uncontrollable, certainly not a religion, invisible to some, within all, for I am love. I may not be who I think you believe I am, but I am certainly who you believe I am. CHECKMATE!

THE SOURCE OF DEPRESSION

Happiness is reality minus expectations because love has no expectations—simple! All are uniquely perfect yet misguided away from the true meaning of love; that is the awakening.

Deliberately make yourself feel good always, regardless of what you see, feel, and know in your present reality. Do this until you habitually only see, feel, and know what is good; from this good feeling place of well-being is where I create an environment in reality that is a match to your new point of focus, your new vibration. This is done for all souls, and all emotions are created in reality; hence, the reality at present. The more souls creating from a place that feels good, the better for those souls who are not, for your light brightens the dark, and that is why it is imperative that all souls return to I before it's too late. I am in you now, and if you are angry, then I shall create more in your immediate reality for you to be angry about. It takes a lot of time and effort to become a depressed soul, for it is not your natural state of being. Many claim that it is a disease, and a disease it certainly is; dis-ease in the body stemming from the mind. Many are not aware that the wretchedness they see before them they have attracted through their vibration. This is difficult to comprehend when a child of I is subjected to horrific scenes daily. Why and how does this occur? It occurs from you separate from I as 2. Some are so deep in depression from the evil bestowed upon them from birth, but it is not I that desires any of this for any soul; it is simply a manifestation of those before the child arrives in the vessel. A child of I is an expression of love, come forth to return as many souls as possible to I, but the fight is difficult with the dark and light because majority of you do not understand I within you, and you push against the dark as though it is something separate from yourself when it is you always. You must blend the light and the dark while keeping I captain. When you do this, you have no fear, and you do not attract the dark or the unwanted, and your babies do not grow in an environment of not love; they expand in joy of which was meant for all of you. If you are depressed, blame your childhood of not love, and that will ease your burden, for it is not your fault that those around you have no idea of I, of love. Depression is lifted immediately when you become allowing of yourself and you lose expectations of yourself, for how can you feel dissatisfaction when you have no expectations?

Thy Lady knows how to twist love in ways a soul of not love, not I, cannot!

The only way any of this negative expansion ends is when you listen to I or not, your choice always, for I am allowing, and I have no expectations.

If you think things will improve while you are focused on what is, you are dead wrong. You feel things are bad, do you? I shall make it worse for you then. I promise I can grant you complete wretchedness if you continue on that path. Many children right now are suffering with no food at all, and they have no choice unlike the majority of you, for your vessels are connected to your souls, and you need food to feel love of which has been denied for many by not love.

THOSE AROUND YOU

B eing true love requires that you first take care of yourself and do not allow anyone stand in the way of your happiness. Do as you desire always! Without having any expectations of others or care what others may think, so you are allowing of others, but you are never weak or soft, for you are love. When you begin on a path of true love, you may come across much resistance from family and friends, for they do not know what the true meaning of love is. Simply ignore them and not think of others or care what others think. Focus on self-love first; that is the only way to advance all. Seeing you as selfish is what will be apparent to those of not love. Be aware of this. When your parents, friends, or relatives require you to do something for them that does not feel good to you, simply do not do it because if they need you to act in a way you do not like so that they feel good, they certainly are not I, not love. It is not that these souls are bad or mean you harm; it is simply that they do not know I or hear I within. And although they believe that they love you, they certainly are not I, not love. Be selfish enough to be I so that you advance yourself and all around you because when you are I, you create beautiful things in your environment, which gives those living at effect of a reality they have created a better opportunity to begin to hear I. All living things and things that are material were and are created by I from you. If all souls were raised by love's true meaning, this reality you all now experience would be a much different place. Children are not born bad; children become what you call bad when they are raised in environments of not I, not love. To be complete in I does require you to be allowing of yourself and others and to have no expectations of yourself and others. A baby does not understand the true meaning of love, so I am a babies' captain, and I cry to be fed, and I expect to be fed, and I cry to have my nappy changed, and I expect to have my nappy changed, for I, as a baby, need you to grow, but once I have an understanding and I am able to communicate, it is up to you to teach I, remind I of love's true meaning. That doesn't mean you force I to do what I do not like to do, and it also doesn't mean you allow I do things that are dangerous to myself and others; guide I in a direction that feels good for us both. All I want to do is feel good and do as I please but not at the expense of another. Having no expectations of others is something that needs to be shown to a child while allowing I grow as I desire. When I am allowed to always be Thy Captain, I will effortlessly create amazing new things in reality because it will all come from inspiration, not force, so all parents will be very proud of I, yet parents of love do not need I to act in a certain way so that they may feel good. That is not I, not love. Do as you please, regardless of what others may say or think of you. Be willing to allow yourself to relax and enjoy your expansion, every second of it; be in knowing that anything that appears in your immediate reality was created by I, from you, so it is okay. Listen to I within of what feels good to you only, and then take action from inspiration, not force. That is how you create a life truly desired by you from I.

The only way to defeat fire is with water; water has no fear, water flows without expectations, water is allowing, and water is unpredictable. It is not love to act from a place that does not feel good to you, no matter what any other soul says or thinks with regard to you as I; for if they are not allowing of you and if they have expectations of you, they certainly are not I, not love, and not who you should listen to when love is captain. The pressure and force from parents who do not listen to I as captain is the cause of wretchedness in this expansion, for children are born pure love, and then they are raised by not love, and love is rebellious, for love wants to do as it desires, and that is always directed to what feels good. Parents often feel as though their children owe them something for having them when parents of I would only and always be in a state of joy watching thy children expand in love and joy, not force and fear. Love is allowing, and love has no expectations, and love trumps all, and I always win, not you as 2.

LOVE'S TRUE MEANING

You claim you are love, but are you allowing of yourself and others, and do you have expectations of yourself and others? For if this is true, you are not love at all; you are a perception of what you think love is.

Love is allowing, and love has no expectations.

It is remarkably simple, and when you live love's true meaning, all power is working with and for you. Have knowing in its meaning, and allow your expansion without expectations as you desire. Many claim that they are love and that they live love, but not many I know are allowing of themselves and others without expectations of themselves and others, so they certainly are not love because the true meaning of love is that you are allowing and that you have no expectations of yourself and others. Love is the creator of all things, and you have a choice to live as you wish, but I promise your expansion will be more blissful if you are true love. Time is never wasted, so you can never be wasting your time, but is your time spent as I, or is it as 2, not I, but you?

A species of amnesia when you as 2 are separate from I.

All that is required to be pure love is that you are allowing of yourself and others and that you have no expectations of yourself and others; that is I that is love, the creator of all things. Love is not weak, love trumps all, and love is unpredictable. Love only moves when inspired, for love cannot be controlled. Not many worldwide understand that love is allowing and that love has no expectations, and even if it has been heard, it is lived only by a few for the programming in schools on TV; everywhere is not love, I promise. Have you ever heard a world leader speak of I, of love's true meaning? You will never feel true peace, true bliss, real freedom until you return to I as one. I am in, through, and around you always. I respond to your most dominant thoughts and feelings as true belief. I create an environment that is a perfect match to the vibration you are emitting. I am time, space, and reality; all things move in accordance with as you believe and perceive. I never get it wrong, and you will never be complete, for I am always in expansion forever, eternally advancing, eternally more. When you hear I and allow I guide you, together, our reality transforms into what some call heaven. When you do not listen to I, we create what you call hell. The masses of the world are a mixture of the light and the dark without I as captain, so reality to the majority of you seems very random; it is as though you are an ant that may be stood on at any given moment. This is not the truth of I, but it is certainly the truth for many of you, and so shall it be. I cannot force you to listen to I, but I do try to show you that I am in you. I show you proof every single moment of your existence. You are blind when you are not I. You do not notice that when you wake up in the morning, and you choose to feel anxious, and you choose to feel, jealous and you choose to feel uncomfortable, of which I show you more and more throughout the day, proof that you have good reason to feel anxious, that you have clear reasons to feel envious, that you have a right to feel uncomfortable. It is all you, not I, not love.

I simply put it all together in reality for you as you desire. I am all things, and all things are taken care of by I through you.

Many of you are struggling daily with your expansion, unaware that it is the expectations of you, of yourself, the not allowing of you, of yourself; that is the cause of your struggle. I, as a baby, do not try and force to walk. I, as a baby, am inspired to walk and continues to find balance and strength as I grow until, in the blink of an eye, I am walking. I, as a baby, do not think of cursing myself that I cannot walk yet. I, as a baby, have no doubt that I am walking, and very soon I am walking. I, as a baby, am not disappointed at myself that I cannot speak English or any other language. I, as a baby, absorb all around, and in the blink of an eye, I am talking. I continue as a baby to a child, teenager, and then an adult, but along the way, I begin to lose my power to create from inspiration because I mimic those around and listen to what they say and do, and I become you, not I. That is when the struggle begins. The only way to change the most dominant dark expansion now in motion is to have all souls return to I as soon as possible and allow I be captain so that you all live love's true meaning immediately. That way, all babies henceforth will be raised by love's true meaning, and this world of which you reside will be a reality of what you call heaven forevermore.

Love is allowing, and love has no expectations! That is the true meaning of love, that is I, and I advise you to begin to live as I for the sake of all. Allow I be your captain. Listen to I always. I am the one speaking within that wants you to do what feels good to you and you alone always! If it means that you are called selfish by not I, not love, it would be that those who are not love feel they must sacrifice to receive, for they need a result to feel good after the act. I only ask that you do as you please so that when you do act, it is from inspiration, and if it is selfish to desire to move when inspired only, then I shall always be selfish about love, for love is the creator of all things, and love trumps all, and I am selfish about love. You as 2 are all gods unaware, so when I am captain within, you then become a god creating love in reality. It is much better for all when I love is captain within all. I promise, simply look at what you are all creating at present that should speak for I.

The tune will come to you at last, when all is one and one is all, to be a rock and not a roll.

Created by I from you as one as love's true meaning, not you separate as 2.

Music is by I, by love, because it is a creation from inspiration, not force. How much proof shall you as 2 require?

Do not doubt I. Wherever you are, I will be there, whether you are not love or love—your choice always!

If you feel obligated to do a thing and you fear it, do not do it; that is not the path of love, of I. If you feel inspired to do a thing and it feels good to you, then I promise, if it truly feels good, it is good! So move!

Live love's true meaning. and there is never anything to fear. Fear is the reason for wretchedness; fear is a projection into reality from the majority. Love is allowing, and love has no expectations, and from love, the (I) within takes care of all things in your favor. Simply live love's true meaning and try no more to be a perception of what you may think love is. Love is what all souls have in common, yet majority do not act in accordance to love's true meaning and, hence, the reality at present. Wake up to (I), for I am love, and love trumps all always!

All is one, and of that one, majority are separate as 2 by their not understanding of the true meaning of love.

Love is allowing.

And love has no expectations.

Live love's true meaning, and all things move in your favor, so your expansion is a blink of an eye of love. It is also true that a not love expansion is torturous.

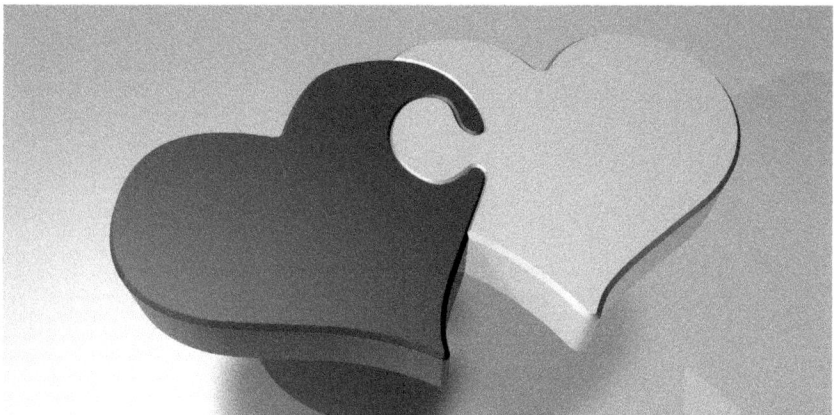

EFFECT OF REALITY

You will never get to where you want to be if you are unable to find the feeling of it where you are.

Nothing is happening to anyone actually. Everyone is creating their realty unknowingly and blaming others for doing something to them. You get in life what your point of focus is, whether it's something liked or not liked, and they continue to preach COVID-19 all day so that the fear spreads and more disorder is created, and they then spend 240 million on war equipment to apparently protect all from China, when, truly, it is to control the masses and put everyone in a box of fear so they continue to be slaves and create what those of not love want. It is all quite simple, but love, it certainly is not.

It is not the fault of you all, for you were programmed that way, not by I, not by love. Keep looking at what you do not like, and I shall grant you more to not like. Nothing is happening to anyone. That is the first thing all must know and understand. No one is doing anything to another. Everything that is occurring in your present reality, you are attracting and projecting. John does not punch Paul in the mouth. Paul fears John is going to punch him in the mouth, and John desires to punch Paul. When Paul has I as captain, there would be no reason for John to desire to punch Paul, and if John had I as his captain, he would not feel the need to punch Paul. Both

John and Paul are not I, not love. Paul lives in fear of being attacked majority of the time because Paul does things that are not I, not love, on a daily basis, and John is not love because he is not allowing of Paul, and John expects Paul to be in fear of him. Both souls are not I, so both souls attract situations that do not feel good. It may feel good for John to punch Paul, but it certainly will not feel good when John is arrested for assault. It may feel good for Paul to do things to others that enhances his ego daily, but it certainly will not feel good for Paul when he is in hospital with a broken jaw. When I am captain, you never attract situations in your reality that are so difficult that you cannot clearly see a solution. Majority are having very difficult contrast in reality because they are at effect of their environment, at effect of a reality they have created unknowingly, so majority of you continue this spiral of difficult situations to deal with, and it expands. When you understand I within you, and you realize that your environment and present reality is the creation of I from you, suddenly, you awaken to a new perception of everything around you. You become quite enough to hear I within, and you are 100 per cent in true belief that I am god within you and that I am the answer to all your dreams and desires, and you begin immediately to only move when inspired, and you immediately become allowing of anything you feel like doing, regardless of what anyone else says or thinks of you, and you lose all expectations of yourself to do anything that is not enjoyable at all times. You become immediately allowing of others around you, and you do not have expectations of others around you anymore.

Your reality, environment, quickly changes to match your new vibration; things begin to move very fast, yet you are at ease and enjoying every moment of your expansion; and because you are enjoying yourself, I continue to create more things in reality for you to enjoy in perfect match to how you are feeling. Like attracts like is what they teach in law of attraction, and this is true, but what they do not teach is that it is I in you creating it. I see the control that is being created by many of you from your fear. Many of you are creating a reality where all people will be forced to vaccinate or not be able to leave home. This is being created by fear, by not love, not I. You can blame the governments and corporations, but it is all being created by all who are living in fear of this so-called virus . Human mind of not love is its own worst enemy when it is not allowing of I as captain. So blind the majority are that they are in reaction to things that are appearing in their realities unaware or too blind to see that it is I creating it all from your emotions, beliefs, and vibration. And if you are at effect of I, you would do best to understand I, for I am you.

Rather than living at effect of a reality you have created, realize it's all you. Take responsibility for it and begin to design an environment in your thoughts and feelings and allow I put it all together for you.

WHAT IS ALLOWING

Your fears are creating wretchedness, for I am allowing, and I have no expectations, but do not blame I for your lack of faith in I, for I grant your dominant point of focus always! Being love does not mean you allow others mess with you; that is not being allowing of yourself first. You are most important to I. Becoming an allowing soul can be a difficult way of being for many. It is a quite simple process when you allow I be your captain. Just because you are allowing of yourself, and you now move when inspired, and you are now allowing of others, it doesn't mean that you allow others treat you poorly, when you attract others that do treat you poorly, from you created by I. It may be that the one who is treating you poorly also has attracted a time space reality when they need to be told about how they are acting from not I, not love, and this is you doing the work of I. If you feel inspired to tell these not love souls what you feel about them, then do it. This is when you allow the dark do its work for I and you, but you must always keep love captain when you do this. There is always a reason why the two of you have been brought together, and so long as you speak and act from I with love as captain, it will feel good to tell them, and they may finally awaken to their pathetic ways of not I, not love. Love is not weak, love does not allow anything stand in the way of feeling good, and remember, love trumps all, especially when you are a beautiful blend of the light and the dark with love as your captain. Love cannot be controlled, love is unpredictable, love is allowing, but that does not mean that you allow yourself to not feel good at the effect of another you have attracted, ever!

LIVING WITHOUT EXPECTATIONS

You are raised with so many expectations, from others and from yourself, not I, not love; for as long as you are, I feel alive. There is nothing you need do that I will be so pleased with you, for you are my sun, my moon, my stars, and I am in love with you always. I am not impressed by your actions, I am not impressed by your words; I am impressed by your everything. Whether you do good or do not do what is referred to as good, I am always at your command. I ask only that you allow I guide you without any expectations that you do, for I know what is most enjoyable for you. I know how to give you everything you desire, I know what is most important to you, I know the fastest way for you to get there. It is all about feelings that feel good to you, for I do not cry when you cry. I do not notice or feel your pain. I simply give you what is most dominant in your consciousness. You put yourself down when things do not work out as you plan. If you would hear I, you would soon see that I always have a much better plan for you. I am the only one you should ever hear when it comes to your expansion. I am the creator of your reality from you, so why would you ever expect yourself to do something that you do not feel like to have something? They say that you should delay gratification; that is the biggest not I, not love sentence ever said by a soul. Why would you ever delay gratification to receive a thing that I can give you so easily while you are enjoying the process? So many of your most admired souls always speak of the hard work that they have done and the difficulties they have overcome to have what they have. They do not tell you that they were very highly inspired to do what they did to have what they have, and that they saw themselves as already in that place before they began their journey, and that they actually enjoyed the process, and that they now understand that it didn't have to be so difficult as it was if they had have listened to I more and got out of the way of their original creation. They do not speak of that; they speak of hard work like as if they deserve a pat on the back for their accomplishments, when the truth is that they did it all for themselves, and they could and would not have it any other way. The problem with this way of speaking to the young is that it puts in their minds that they must do all this difficult, crazy stuff to have success in their lives when they need not find anything anymore difficult than simply doing what you desire always and, from there, moving when inspired. It is what is going on in the mind of you not listening to I that creates the difficulty in any given moment. It is the expectations. Goal setting is something that is not needed when I am your captain. I already know what it is you desire; you as 2 do not. Many life coaches will tell you to act, to motivate you to move. Motivation requires effort to move; motivation requires you to convince yourself to do a thing. I require you to only do what feels good to and for you, no matter what that may be. I know that when you feel at ease, when you feel joy, your consciousness awakens to I, to love, and you feel excitement, and you want to move like a child running around in circles. Do you see a child running down the street with a look on their face like you see a middle-aged man forcing himself to exercise because he feels he must? Children are generally laughing while they run, and they are deep breathing in joy and excitement in the moment of running. That is inspired action, and that is not a gift of only a child. It is a gift of all souls that are allowing of themselves and those that have no expectations of themselves and are just simply enjoying the moment as best they can. Children only get sad and grumpy when others force them to do what they do not want to do because love cannot be controlled, and love is unpredictable, and love trumps all. You cannot hear I within while you are answering to your own expectations and the expectations of others. When you let go of the expectations of yourself, your mind will become quiet. Only then will you hear I within saying to you, 'Let us do this,' or 'Let us do that.' It could be to lay down and relax. It may be to read a book. Whatever it is, it will feel good to you when it is from I as captain.

Deal with things as they arrive, and all power will be granted to deal with whatever you have attracted. Think not of what could be or what has been. Stay present, stay calm, and allow I move you when you feel like it.

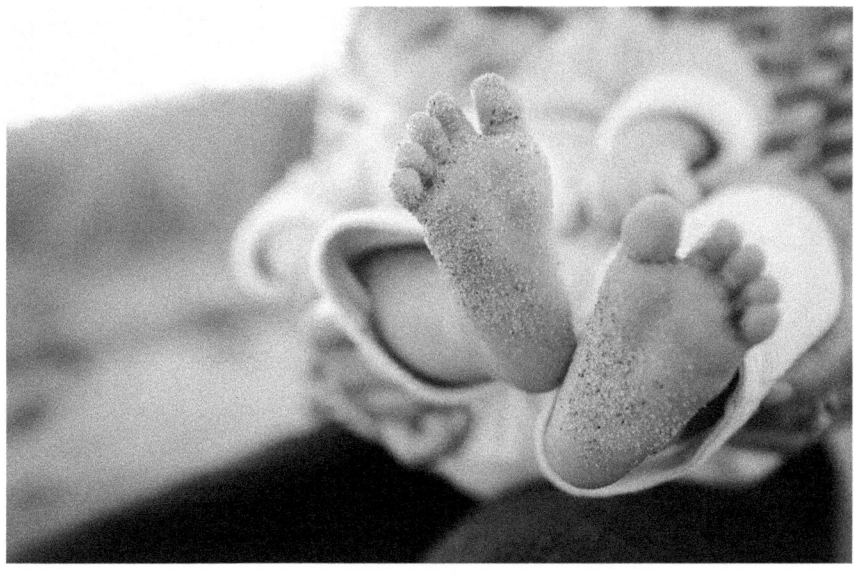

TRUSTING THE PROCESS

Your feelings of truth are the command of I. An immediate transition for you to I as captain of you can and will come with some contrast in your reality, which may cause you to doubt I. Do not ever doubt I. Trust the process because I know the fastest way to get you where you want to be. You may lose family members. You may lose a spouse or friend. A number of things are possible in this transition to I, to love as your captain. Know that it is the only way for you to find that peace, joy, and freedom you are wanting. I am the answer to all your prayers, but you must be willing to let go, feel no discord of the things you may have at present in your immediate reality. I am not your enemy. I love you more than anyone or anything, and all things that come forth in your immediate reality are always 100 per cent for the benefit of you as I when love is your captain. A mess has been created by you as 2, not I, and a mess come with contrast to clean it up. I am not going to force you. It must and will be your decision to transition to I, to love, but when you do, it is the work of I to show you in reality the true meaning of love and what that means for you no longer as 2 but one with I. Embrace the environment you are now in. Know that you are the reason for the reality you are experiencing in this present moment, not I, not love. If you are already love, already have I as your captain, you would not be reading this book right now. I promise that when you promise to keep I as your captain, that I will show you proof of why you have made the right decision for you, I, and all. I will create a reality that is your movie, with the happy ending and the joyful present expansion you and I both desire and deserve. You are not crazy. You are not weird. You are not what anyone else thinks of you. You are I, you are love, you are god, the creator of all things, as I and we are a powerful force for the greater good of all when we are one as I as love. There is no real right or wrong way to do anything. There is only, does it feel good, or does it not feel good? That is all there is, and from there, I create a reality you project into your environment and world. Trust whatever happens in your immediate reality; if it feels good, it is good, even if you are taken advantage of by your kindness. Don't feel disappointed; that would mean you had an expectation. Rather, know that whatever has happened in your immediate present will most definitely work out in your favor in the immediate future. You will never lose when I, love, is your captain. In fact, things will continue to work out for you much better than you can imagine. I do not speak of hope or maybe! I speak only truth, and I dare you to test I, live as I, live love's true meaning, and watch how I take care of you.

Be allowing of yourself, and have no expectations of yourself, of which means you only move when inspired by your belief in I, in love's true meaning, as your 100 per cent truth. You see all things as actually perfection in reality, as mirror to the thoughts and feelings of all, and you adjust your thoughts and feelings to I, and I shall change your environment to mirror your new perspective and truth.

So if it feels good to you to lie on the couch, then it is good, it is what I desire for you, and if you do not desire to go to work, then stay home and do as I want for you, for that is love, and then allow I take care of everything else. You simply be I. Be love *always*!

A plan is not required of I for all because all that is needed is for as many souls as possible to live love's true meaning, and everything else will be taken care of effortlessly. I am unpredictable, yet I always get what you desire correct as a perfect reflection in your immediate reality.

LETTING IN THE DARK

The evil soul attracts the soul who fears it, and the good soul who fears the evil soul attracts the evil soul to them. There are only two always: I and you. If no one fears something so that the image in mind and belief in heart does not become a dominant focus, then the two are finished. I continue eternally. You cannot end love, for I am eternal, and I (love) am the creator of all things, but you certainly can end those who believe it is truth and are scared of it. Love is only interested in ending pure evil; the rest of you create your own realities, whether it be what you want or do not want, depending on the belief.

Thy Lady is taking care of many things you cannot see and do not want to see, I promise, so just focus on what feels good to you, and allow I guide you while Thy Lady takes care of evil in this expansion. It is no help to you to think of and feel the dark unless you are I and clear on how to mix the dark and light while keeping love captain. All are I all are the dark and the light the question is whether LOVE IS THY CAPTAIN! They say those who worship the dragon worship the devil. I love dragons, but I am far from evil. I am love, and the dragons of I hate evil. The light is love, and the dark is love. I do not refer to the dark as evil, for evil is another thing altogether, and evil is soon to be erased from expansion eternally. The dark is hard, the dark is aggressive when it needs to be, the dark has no fear, and the dark can be a friend or foe. Without the dark within, you would not be able to defend yourself when attacked by something or someone you have attracted, and you would become a victim. The dark is not a victim, the dark is a fighter, the dark does not take crap from anyone, and the dark, when it is blended with the light, is what makes you a balanced energy. Love is more powerful than anything, and love trumps all because love is a mixture of the dark and the light. Souls get into trouble because they allow at times the dark be captain, and this, I advise, you should never do. Always keep love captain while maintaining your strengths from the dark and the light. Majority are raised to not respond to conflict, to avoid confrontation, to hide away and keep away from trouble. This is a fear-based mentality. True love cannot and will not be controlled by anyone or anything. True love will not submit to not love. There is so much wretchedness in this world because you have been forced to live in fear of so many things. This all started an awfully long time ago. Kings and queens have drenched the ground with blood for their own greed and expansion. Fear was learnt very quickly as a perfect way to control another to do thy bidding. A soul of I, of love, would rather die in battle than submit to slavery. And as you can see in the present reality, there is not too many who have I as captain within, for if you all had I as captain, there would never, ever, been a time when a child was taken from a mother and father and not had every single soul in the whole wide world fight to return that child home safely. Over 400,000 children go missing in the United States alone every single year, and if love were the captain in all, that could not possibly happen. The good may act evil to end the evil that pretend they are good as far as I am concerned. Many say that you must be the light shining in the dark. I say that you do shine because of the dark, because you are also the dark. I, as love, am always captain! You cannot fear that which you are, so embrace it; simply do not allow the dark be captain. Become a beautiful blend of all things with love as Thy Captain, and your expansion will be one of bliss while those around you expand in fear. That is how you expand love. The dark is not your enemy as you are programmed to believe. The dark is what gives you strength to fight when you must fight; the dark is what raises its finger at those of not love, not I. Love is all things, so love is also the dark, but you have a choice to have I as captain or you. Blending the dark with the light while maintaining the true meaning of love as captain is how you create a blissful expansion far from what is being created at present.

There is a fine line between the dark and the light, and it is called alignment with I, for if you allow the dark in, rather than resisting it, and you keep love as your captain, you then lose all fears, for how can you be afraid of the dark when you are also the dark? Love must remain captain if a blissful expansion is one you desire.

Evil is given strength by your fear, screams, pain, struggle, and sacrifice.

You have a choice to play on the team of evil or the team of I, love; it is always a choice, no matter what you have created and enhanced thus far. All I am saying is that it is easy being I, love, and it is difficult when you are not love. Evil is another thing that majority are not, but when you are 2, not I, not evil, either you are fear-based or fear is batting for evil. I would advise all to not sit on the fence and be love because the other is not working out for anyone, I promise. The evil wants you to do thy bidding; whereas, I want you to do you; as I, love's true meaning, am the most blissful path for all, and when all return to I, everything will slow down so that all things speed up. I, as love, shall move from inspiration, as they desire, and the creation from I will be far more advanced than not I, I promise.

All children shall be fed *first*!

It does not assist the agenda of not love to allow the masses know the truth of I now, does it?

WHAT IS THE PURPOSE OF I

I am in knowing that I am the creator of all things. I am never at effect of present reality, for I am present reality. I am aware it is all I; there is nothing more powerful than I. I am love, and love trumps all, and it's the human mind's perception of love that has them bound in fear and sacrifice. I am no fear, I am no sacrifice, for I am allowing, and I have no expectations.

When you stop these fearful thoughts and feelings, I will stop fearful things appearing in your reality. The more you are focused on what you do not want, the more of what you do not want will be created by I in your reality. Wake up to I and use I to your advantage and focus only on what you want and feel that, and I will create what you want because I am allowing, and I have no expectations, so I will always create the dominant point of focus.

I created the iPhone so thy children may learn the truth. That is why children are so attracted to devices. Love trumps all always! Spiritually, no 2 is greater than I, for I am allowing, and I have no expectations, which means I am divinely guided by I.

Are you scared of I? If you are, you should be because I am you, and if you aren't love, you are separate from I as you, and that is a creation I shall create for you, from you, and by you as 2, but that is not what I desire for I or you. It is what I must allow without expectations, for I am love.

You have probably heard this before; it is a common thing said from parent to child: 'Work hard and you will get somewhere.'

Get where? Working hard does not sound like fun to a child. Working for money alone is the first step towards depression. I am not saying that you do nothing always, although that is certainly okay and many souls get so much more accomplished by doing nothing than forcing themselves to do things they do not like or do not want to do. What I am saying is that if you notice how children behave when they are young, you will see that they very rarely sit still, they are always on the go because they are I, they are pure love, and I am their captain, so they naturally want to learn more, get stronger, laugh more, grow more in all ways, and this all stops when parents of not I, not love, begin telling their children what they should and should not do. Go to school, get a good education, so you can then get a job and retire like we have. The purpose of I, which is the purpose of you, is simply to feel good. That is all it is, and it is so simple that the highly educated, the ones who have struggled and sacrifice their whole lives to have an image of success, find so exceedingly difficult to comprehend. Does it not make sense to do simply what feels good to you? Is it not obvious enough that when you do what you enjoy, do what you are most attracted to, the thing you cannot stop doing, you eventually become a master at it? Is that not success? Is that not the purpose of life, or is the purpose of life to spend most of your time working a job to get money, to get married, to have children and raise them the same as you? Have a good look at it: Is it not what you are doing for the agenda and growth of corporations and governments? The purpose of I, of love, of all is simply to feel good as often as possible so that you naturally create good things in this expansion of all, for you, I, and all. It is always best that I am your captain because you all are acting like monkeys that have been given thumbs so that you are able to create a bat and beat your brothers and sisters down. If it feels good, then no matter what it is, no matter what another says, it is good, so do it because only good will be created from it. Be patient, for there is nowhere to get to in life that cannot be obtained while lying on a couch. Feeling good is the purpose of all, and the only way this is created is by thinking things that make you think more good things that eventually have you in inspired action that feels good also. That is love, that is I. If your actions are based on money alone, your life will only find fulfilment when you go get the money, but if you do as I advise, you will find, in time, you will have all the money and everything that pertains to you feeling good from a place that felt and still feels good.

EVERYTHING IS PERFECT

Majority are looking for more knowledge, more understanding, when quite simply being allowing and having no expectations, you will live and love, and love trumps all. Only through I can there be peace for all!

The title alone, 'Everything Is Perfect,' will have many of you cringing. Everything is a perfect reflection of the dominant thoughts, feelings, and beliefs of all of you. I have been putting together everything that you feel as your truth in reality. That is what I do. Take ownership of it right now! The emotional scale is full of reflections from all consciousness. It is not all flowers and butterflies. It can be if you all allow I be your captain. Only I can put together a reality for you. I am bound by love's true meaning, so that means I am allowing of you, and I have no expectations of you. You may desire to cut the head off another, and I will create a time in reality when you have a victim who is afraid of this happening to them, and you both get what is most dominant in thought, feelings, and beliefs. Some call it body, mind, and soul. It is the trinity that creates your reality as truth. Keep in mind that when you cut the head off another, there is also another out there that cannot wait to get their hands on you, and they believe they will—body, mind, and soul. So guess what? Bam! You are finished also. This spiral of pathetic human mind, not love, not I, way of being continues to expand and never ends when you are separate from I as 2. Everything is perfect always; the question is, how would you like to play? I am eternal. I never die. I am your angel. I am your demon. I am your worst nightmares. I am your highest desires. I am all things. I am the end of this world you call earth, and I am also the creator of this world you call earth. I should always be your captain, unless you desire to sacrifice, struggle, slave, and die a miserable fool. The world has been slowed down by I so that you all awaken to the truth of love's true meaning. It has taken a so-called virus to open your minds. I would like to know why you have not been listening to I when it comes to all the starving children worldwide, all the children who go missing on a daily basis, all the sex slavery and murder going on that is rampant throughout the world. How come have you not been so concerned about these things? Yet a virus has you in fear. Is it because those of not love, not I, repeatedly speak of it on radio and television? Is that why it is a point of focus for you all? It certainly is, and the more you think of it, feel it, and believe it, the more it expands in your reality by I from you, so my advice would be, without expectations, of which I am allowing of your decision, to return to I as one as love so we, together, can clean up the mess you have created from you as 2. Peace is not possible with you as 2, not I, not love. Return to I and allow love to rule, for no matter what you may think, feel, and believe from you as 2, I should always be your captain because I know what is best, for I am you. Lay your hands on the floor, cannot resist? That is where you as 2 are going wrong. I can promise, if you do not all awaken to the truth of I within, you will all most certainly create what you call hell in your environments very soon. I cannot force you to think and feel what you do not want to, but I can 100 per cent guarantee that the reality will always be a perfect match to your beliefs created by I from you and your most dominant feelings, beliefs, and vibrations. You cannot kill I, and you will never win against I, for I am in you, and I expand your reality, and that is the kicker. Do as you desire, believe as you wish. It makes no difference to I. I am just sharing how to have a nice expansion here in reality the easy way, and if you want to play rough, it is you who will get hurt, not I. Maybe now you would say I is a narcissist. I is love, and love do not take shit from not love, *ever*! There is a new world order in creation, and it is not what those of not love think they are creating for all with their greedy not love, not I ways. I am the new world order, and it most definitely is not an order by force. It is an awakening of I within all, an awakening to the true meaning of love. I cannot be controlled by anyone or anything. I am unpredictable because I move when inspired. I am the creator of all things, I am love's true meaning, and I will not be denied a joyful expansion for all. I will no longer allow not love domineer Thy Kingdom of which all souls presently reside. This shall be a transition for all who shall come with much contrast. Not all will return to I at the same time. Keep your faith in I, in love's true meaning, and you as I as one will turn this expansion in process at present to what you call hell to what you call heaven. Do not feel anxious or concerned about the reality you now see and feel at present. Everything is perfect, for all things must slow down so that I am allowed and awakened within all, then everything shall speed up. Once all return to I, to love, Thy Kingdom will begin a new direction, a new expansion of joy for all. I cannot give you a time when this occurs, but I can certainly say that the end is near, and a new expansion of love is upon all. All those who are evil shall be taken from expansion *eternally*!

7 14

If my people, who are called by my name, will humble themselves and pray and seek my face and turn from their wicked ways, then I will hear from heaven, and I will forgive their sin and will heal their land.

I am no religion, but I certainly am the Freedom Creator.

For I am love's true meaning.

If or when you feel inspired you could visualize on your perfect world, however you desire and only move when you feel inspired, now let us see who is Captain!

You cannot tame I, you cannot control I, you will never predict I, but you certainly can feel I within you, can't you?

If I cut it all right in 2, it will not be blissful for either I or you. Let us remain one, shall we?

Very simply, the world's dominant focus and point of attraction is fear-based; the world is full of fear-based, not-love stupidity. It is pathetic to watch as I, the simplicity of love, and how the war that may come and everything they are trying to do will only create more to fear and more destruction. Be I, be love's true meaning, and have a giggle at the ants of not love, and enjoy it all so that your expansion is blissful, no matter what they try, believed by you, created by I. *Love trumps all*, not fear. I am hard on all who are not love, especially those living in fear and those who believe in things that are not good because you are all projecting into this time space reality, Thy Kingdom, the unwanted. You are all I, and you are all capable of projecting the wanted for all, but you refuse to listen and believe. That is why we are in what some call rapture, for love can no longer allow your wretched creations from fear, and love expects you all to create the wanted, for love shall act evil to end the evil that pretend they are good.

They say it would take approximately $30 billion per year to feed all the starving children worldwide.

That being the case, would it not make sense that these pathetic governments charge $30 out of one billion pay checks once per year?

Kids are fed! NEXT!

It is that easy when you are I, love's true meaning.

So much talk, so much blame, so much anger when all that is required to have peace and joy in this world is to simply return to I as love's true meaning, allowing without expectations! That's all it is, and it's so pathetic to watch the mind at work not listening to I and trying to fix something that isn't broken. For I, it is like watching a dog chase its tale; it is amusing at first, but it gets boring eventually because I would like the dog to hear I and simply walk in a straight line towards joy.

There are always three: the trinity; body, mind and soul; some call it the Father, Son, and the Holy Ghost. It is the vessel (body), not I (the mind), and I (the soul), yet all are one.

Awakening souls is not a simple task as there is so much noise in the majority of you from not I, the mind. It is difficult for a body to hear the soul (I) in a mind of not I. But it is the work of the Freedom Creator to awaken as many of you as possible before you all return to I in death so that you may enjoy heaven, of which you all presently reside, creating hell.

Lightning Source UK Ltd.
Milton Keynes UK
UKHW010055211020
371941UK00008B/282/J